A SUBTLE ALLEGORY CONCERNING THE SECRETS OF ALCHEMY

Very Useful to Possess
and Pleasant to Read

MICHAEL MAIER

WITH EDWARD CLARY

The Alchemical Press

The Secrets of Alchemy – Copyright © 1984, 2001 by Holmes Publishing Group LLC. Corrections are copyrighted by Edward Clary. All rights reserved. No part of this book may be reproduced or utilized in any form or by any means, electronic or mechanical, including photocopying, recording or by any information storage and retrieval system, without permission in writing from Holmes Publishing Group except in the case of brief quotations embodied in critical articles and reviews.

ISBN 0-916411-17-6

SECOND EDITION,

REVISED

— 2001 —

HOLMES PUBLISHING GROUP LLC
POSTAL BOX 2370
SEQUIM WA 98382 USA

THE SECRETS OF ALCHEMY

After spending the best part of my life in the study of the liberal arts and sciences, and in the company of wise men and judicious scholars, I was compelled, as the result of my observation of mankind, to arrive at the melancholy conclusion that the hearts of most persons are set either on ambitious and vainglorious projects, on sensual pleasures, or on the accumulation of wealth by all and any means; and that few care either for God or for virtue. At first I did not quite know whether to become a disciple of the laughing or of the weeping philosopher, or whether to join in the exclamation of the wise Prince of Israel: "All things are vanity." But at length the Bible and experience taught me to take refuge in the study of the hidden secrets of Nature, whether pursued at home, by means of books or abroad, in the Great Volume of the World. Now, the more I drank of the mighty fount of knowledge, the more painfully my thirst, like that of Tantalus, seemed to increase. I had heard that there was a bird called Phoenix, the only one of its kind in the whole world, whose feathers and flesh constitute the great and glorious medicine for all passion, pain, and sorrow; which also Helena, after her return from Troy, had presented in the form of a draught to Telemachus, who thereupon had forgotten all his sorrows and troubles. This bird I could not indeed hope to obtain entire, but I was seized with an irresistible longing to become possessed of at least one of its smallest feathers; and for this unspeakable privilege I was prepared to spend all my substance, to travel far and wide, and to endure every hardship. There was, of course, much to discourage me. Some people denied the very existence of this bird; others laughed at my faith in its wonder-working properties. I was thus brought for a time to regard all that Tacitus, Pliny, and all other writers have said as fabulous, and to doubt whether, after all, the different narcotics and opiates were not a better remedy for anger and sorrow than the supposed virtues of the Phoenix. Moreover, I had heard of the simple method of curing these mental ailments suggested by a certain wise man to Augustus, whom he bade run through the twenty-four letters before saying anything whenever he was angry; and this suggestion appeared to supersede all other remedies. I had also read the books of those moral philosophers who undertake to prescribe an effective remedy for every disease of the mind. But after giving all these boasted specifics a fair trial, I found, to my dismay, that they were of little practical use. In many cases, the causes of mental maladies appeared to be material, and to consist in an excess or defect of the bile, or of some other bodily substance; in all these cases a medical treatment seemed to be indicated; whence Galen, that prince among physicians, was led to believe that character depends on temperaments of the body. As a soldier may lose all his bravery and strength by being starved and confined in a close prison, so even a good person may yield to anger, simply through some vicious habit of body. This opinion is most reasonable in itself, and is borne out, amongst other things, by the testimony which is given by Arnold of Villanova, in that book of his where he sets forth the virtues of all medicines by means of tables of the four qualities: "The medicines that conduce to intellectual excellence are those which strengthen the digestion, and nourish the brain and the principal vitals, purging out all superfluities, purifying the blood, and preventing the ascent of vapours to the brain; hence you will find that many medical writers speak of their medicines as productive of a direct effect upon the mind, when it is only through the medium of the stomach, the brain, the blood, the liver, etc., that they tend to brighten the intellectual faculties, by improving the general health of the brain, and quickening all processes of the body, that you may say they are productive of joy, because they tend to strengthen the chief limbs, purify the blood, and produce good animal spirits. Other medicines "lead to Paradise," as they dispose the heart to charity and to every good work by their action upon the blood. Some medicinal herbs have the power of exciting love, by increasing and clarifying the blood, and thus quickening the sexual instinct; while others make men chaste and religious, by inducing poverty and frigidity of blood, and taking away the edge of all sensual appetite. In the same way, it is possible, by means of certain drugs, to make men stupid and insane, as men are rendered dull and stolid by drinking too much wine. You may also notice, sometimes, that after eating a certain kind of food, men become light-hearted, joyous, and inclined to dance and sing—though they are ordinarily staid and grave persons—while other kinds of food have a contrary effect upon them. Thus, a physician has the power to make a miser liberal, a chaste person lascivious, a timid person bold, simply by changing the complexion of his vital juices. Such are the wonderful secrets of the Medical Art, though of course, they are hidden from the foolish and the ignorant. There are a great many infatuated persons who will not believe that medicine can do anything but cure a headache; but such people know little of the resources of this science. Hippocrates forbade the physicians whom he taught to reveal these secrets; and it was a wise prohibition. A little further on the same writer says: "What medicine can produce greater heat than anger? or chill the body more than fear? or invigorate the nerves more thoroughly than joy? or nourish and comfort more gently than hope? And what more certain cause of death is there than despair?" These are the words of the philosopher, and they shew that medicine may, through the body, cure the mind, and thus supply a remedy for anger as well as other mental disturbances. It is true that if there is a remedy for anger, it would, in the present state of the world, hardly be very highly esteemed. Suntil it would calm the passions of individuals, although other persons might not recognise its value. But that which men do not care to have just now, may one day be in great demand. Such is the vicissitude of all things human. Galen once said that the savages of England and Germany were as hostile to the science of Medicine as they were ignorant of it. But now the descendants of Galen's countrymen are sunk in barbarism, while the English and Germans are the most skillful physicians in the world. Thus it seems very likely that this remedy may be one day in great request, especially when we consider its vast utility, and the innumerable evils which anger brings upon men.

What has been said about anger applies with equal force to grief; for while the symptoms of anger are more or less mental, those of grief produce a more perceptible and lasting effect on the body. This great remedy for anger and grief, then, it would be most desirable to have, if we could only find the Phoenix which affords it. Where shall I look for it? Where shall I inquire after it? Whom shall I ask? I determined to go abroad, and to search for it until I should have found it. Fortune assists the brave: to the indolent and idle knowledge never comes. I would leave my native country—dearly as I love it, and sadly as I should miss my friends—and wander from land to land until I should be able to return with the eagerly coveted Medicine. All beginnings are difficult: he who has never been sad, cannot rejoice; he who has never erred, cannot be brought back to the right way; and as the Chemists say: "There is in Alchemy a certain noble body, which is moved from master to master, whose beginning is misery and sourness, whose end is sweetness and joy." So I expected to endure hardships, and go through bitter experiences, but I also expected them to be crowned with the delights of success. Of the existence of the Phoenix I had no doubt or I could not have looked for it. It is enough for me to see the Sun and its rays, even though I cannot touch it; and perhaps it is as well for us that we cannot get so very close to the Sun. But as to this Medicine which I seek; how can I have a perfect knowledge of it before I see and touch it? How can I become a Master before I have been a scholar? The products of all countries are not the same; and perhaps I may learn in one part of the world what I cannot get to know in another. Moreover, I asked myself the question: Can a pilgrim's life hurt any one? Are we not all pilgrims here below to that land whither our Saviour Christ has gone before? And is not the example of peregrination set us by the swallow, the herald of spring by the crane, the stork, and other birds of passage? Does not the whole world lie open before man as the air is everywhere accessible to birds? Great Phoebus himself, the god of the Sun, journeys day by day over the wide expanse of the sky. The heart of man beats and pulsates in his bosom from the first to the last hour of his life; and being surrounded by all these models and examples, it is natural for man to lead the life of a pilgrim, particularly if that pilgrimage be directed towards a certain goal. The merchant travels over land and sea to buy the produce of distant climes; but a nobler merchandise by far are science and knowledge, which are the wares of the mind. He who stays at home will there bury his talents, and get to know little about the secrets of the universe. Moreover, it is both pleasant to travel and honourable to be always several hours' journey in advance of the Sun. That which is most spiritual is most swift in its movements, while the lifeless earth alone is immovable. The other three elements are in perpetual motion: the air sweeps over the earth in the shape of winds, hurricanes and gales; fire devours everything before it as it rushes onward in the conflagration of a great city; water runs along in rivers and mighty streams, and hastens to reach the sea. Let us also look up and behold the heavens as they move in their glory. The stars, the sun, and the moon know the times and seasons of their rising and setting. A cannon ball, if projected from one of our most powerful guns, would be more than eight days in making the compass of the world (which is more than 25,000 miles); but the Sun, notwithstanding its vast size, accomplishes the same distance in 24 hours. It would make our thoughts reel if we strove to realise the velocity with which Saturn moves round the Sun, and with which the heavens revolve round their own axis. But greater suntil, and far more wonderful, is the speed of human thought, which, in a moment of time, travels from one end of the heavens to the other. We may believe that the angels, as spiritual beings, move with the quickness of that which is spiritual in man, viz. thought. God alone does not move; for He is everywhere. For all these reasons, I conceived that it would be both interesting, pleasant, honourable, and eminently profitable for me to follow the example of the whole world, and to undertake a pilgrimage for the purpose of discovering this wonderful bird Phoenix. I therefore braced myself for a long journey, determining to travel. first, through all the countries of Europe, then, if necessary, to America, thence to Asia, and at last to pass on to Africa. If, after carefully searching for the Phoenix in all these parts of the world, I did not succeed in finding it or hearing of it, I might reasonably give up all hopes of ever setting eyes thereon. The plan of my journey was determined by the relative quality of the elements which the different parts of the world represent, i.e., Europe stands for earth, America for water, Asia for air, and Africa for fire. Earth cannot become air except through the medium of water; nor can water become fire except through the medium of air. I determined, then, to go first to Europe, which represents the grossest, and last to Africa, which represents the most subtle element. But my reasons will be set forth more clearly as I come to speak of the different parts of the world.

EUROPE: EARTH

I left my native town on the day of the vernal equinox, when the Moon and Sun were both in the sign of Aries, with the intention of first travelling through Europe, and to inquire everywhere after the Phoenix. I took Europe to represent the element Earth, because earth forms the foundation of all the ether elements, and stands out above the water, so Europe is the mother of the whole world, and though smaller than other continents, is vastly superior to them through the courage, energy, and mental strength of its inhabitants. Some say that one handful of earth gives ten handfuls of water, a hundred handfuls of air, and a thousand handfuls of fire; and this is the relative importance of the different continents, if Europe answers to earth. Europe has produced the bravest warriors, and the most distinguished conquerors; and though she has subdued other continents, she has herself never been subjugated by them. Of the four great world empires, only one was founded by an Asiatic prince; the Macedonian, the Roman, and the Teutonic Empires, have all had their centres in Europe. Alexander the Great and Julius Caesar were among her sons. If we look at a map of Europe we may easily perceive that in shape this part of the world resembles a virgin; but her heart is that of a lion. For these reasons, I determined to travel first through this Virgin Lion, because it clearly corresponds to the fundamental element: earth.

Europe is a Virgin because of her beauty and spotless purity; a Lion because she has conquered others, but has never herself been conquered. Among the heavenly bodies the Sun answers to Europe, and among the metals, gold. For though she produces little gold, and the sun shines upon her with less fierceness than on Africa, yet she is worthy of being compared to the Sun and gold because of the excellence of her people, though a few years ago even some real lions were born in Germany, yet we call her a Lioness only on account of her stoutness of heart. Europe is the Mother of the World, and Germany is her heart.

Nor is Europe without her marvels. In Pannonia, it is reported, men live in compact stone houses under water. The hot springs of Carlsbad, it is said, are hardened into stones. On the coasts of Prussia, a transparent and pellucid stone (amber), formed out of subterraneous vegetable juices, is cast ashore in large quantities. I do not mention the coral of the Sicilian sea, which, originally a plant, hardens outside water into a white or red tree of stone, or the sealed earth of Germany and Silesia... Europe then, is the Lion Earth. This expression is for those who hear not with their ears only but also with their brains, it is earth which resists the fire, like gold, and is not resolved into air. Like the boundary pillar of the gods of old, it "yields to none." Hence Europe (the gold of the universe) seemed the very place in which I should be most likely to hear of the Phoenix and its Medicines but most of those whom I met laughed at my quest, and said that, like Narcissus, I had fallen in love with the shadow of my own mind, the echo of my vain and ambitious thoughts, which had no substantial existence apart from my own folly. "The words of the Alchemists," said they, "are like clouds." They may mean and represent anything, according to the fancy of him who hears them. And even if there were such a Medicine, human life is too brief for the search, all that makes life worth living will have to be neglected and thrust aside while you are engaged in the hunting after it. If we can pick up a knowledge of this secret casually, and whilst devoting ourselves to other pursuits, well; but if not, we can very ill spare the time for a closer search." These objections (at least the latter half of them) I met as follows: "The quest of this Medicine demands the whole powers of a man's body and mind. He who engages in it only casually, cannot hope to penetrate even the outward rind of knowledge. The object of our search is a profound secret, and a man who is not prepared to give himself wholly to this inquiry had much better abstain from it altogether. I readily acknowledge that the powers of my mind are not such as to justify me in anticipating success. But the spirit within me impels me to undertake this search; and I am confident that God will at the last reward my patience, and my humble waiting upon Him. As every King loves his Queen, as every bridegroom is devoted to his bride, so I regard this science as more beautiful and lovely than anything else in the world besides now, beautiful things are hard to win, and hard toil is the way to all that is great and glorious." This was the gist of my answer. Now I had already travelled through a great part of Europe, when it occurred to me that Italy and Spain are constantly mentioned by the Ancients as the great seats of secret knowledge, and I therefore directed my steps thitherward. In Spain I heard that some Arabs (Geber, Avicenna, and others) had lived there a long time ago, and these had possessed the wonderful Medicine; I was also told a great deal about Hercules and his achievement in securing the golden apples of the Hesperides, and also the golden cup, wherein he received the Medicine for anger and sorrow. Now all prudent men have decided that it contained a small portion of the feathers of the Phoenix. I saw that Geryon with the three bodies was the theme of the philosopher's writings, that Hercules was a laborious artist, seeker of the Medicine. But nobody was able to give me any definite information. I did not, however, wish to leave Europe without visiting the Canary Islands, which are seven in number and are named: Lancerotta, Bonaventura, Great Canaria, Teneriffe, Gomera, Ferro, and Palma. Three of them, Lancerotta, Gomera, and Ferro, are governed each by its own King. Ferro is naturally destitute of good drinking water, but the inhabitants get a supply of it out of certain broad-leaved trees, which disuntil sweet water in such quantities as to suffice for the whole island. Strangers and pirates who land in the island, being ignorant of this fact, are prevented by want of water from staying in Ferro very long. Now, it happened about this time that the King of Gomera had died without leaving a male heir, and his subjects refused to acknowledge the authority of his beautiful daughter Blanche, unless she accepted the hand of some royal wooer, because they said that it was unworthy of men to be ruled by a woman, and calculated to injure the manliness of the national character—as was shewn by the experience of those peoples over whom women have borne sway for any length of time. For there women had assumed the place of men, while men were degraded to the position of women; and, as a consequence, there followed the wildest excesses of profligacy and lewdness. So the royal maiden was prevailed upon to think of bestowing her hand in marriage. Now, there was in the island a royal youth, named Brumazar (with beautiful dark locks and a splendid golden robe), who was passionately enamoured of the royal maiden Blanche, and was loved by her in return. He wooed and won her, and the wedding was celebrated on condition that she should bring to him as her dower a diamond of great value and magnitude, while he should present to her a splendid ruby of incalculable worth (i.e., worth a million ducats); he, as her King and Lord, should protect her from all dangers and from the robbers with whom that country swarms, while she, on the other hand, promised humbly to obey him without either subterfuge or tergiversation. After these preliminaries, they were linked together in close and indissoluble marriage, in which they lived long and happily; and it was predicted that a son should be born to them, who would be a mighty conqueror, and would carry his victorious arms as far as the Pillars of Dionysus in India... So you see that I was unable to get any information whatsoever about the Phoenix in the course of my wanderings through Europe; I therefore determined to set sail for America, in the hope that I might be more fortunate among the savages of that Continent For I remembered the words of the poet:—

"Accident is a mighty helper;
let your hook always be baited;
in the least likely river you may catch your fish."

AMERICA: WATER

In these days, when commerce has opened up, as it were, a highroad across the seas to America (or India in the West), there is no very great difficulty in reaching that continent; but far different were the circumstances under which it was first discovered. After leaving the "Islands of the Blessed," I became a passenger on board a ship which had an eagle for its figurehead; and, after weathering many severe gales and hurricanes, we at length landed in Brazil, a great province of America, entirely covered with forests. The surface of the country is only dotted here and there with the homestead of a settler; there are few towns, and the inhabitants are sunk in ignorance, and unskilled in the arts of civilisation. How, then, could I hope to hear anything about the Phoenix among people who could hardly read or write? Yet there are in this country many rare and beautiful birds which are not found elsewhere, though, of course, the Phoenix, being a miraculous bird, must not be sought among common fowls. The trees of the land are of a rich colour and sweet fragrance; and one day when I was enjoying the wild beauty of the forest, and listening to the natural music of the birds, I happened to find an apple of unusual and exquisite beauty, which on a closer view exhibited the following inscription:—

Within is that which, if you deliver it to its grandmother,
there will thence arise a son who may cling to his mother
in loving embrace.
From this union will arise in a short time a noble tree
which will render to the husbandman a golden harvest.

After much thinking, it occurred to me that the seed which was in the fruit must be placed in the earth (its grandmother, since the parent tree was its mother). So I took it as a gift of God, sowed the seed, and when there had sprung up a little tree, I grafted it into the parent tree (first having sawn off that tree close to the ground) and when the two had grown together, they became a much more glorious tree than either of them had been before, and the fruit was that of the scion which had been inserted into the parent tree.... It is said that before the Spaniards reached Brazil, there were no horses in that country, so that the natives regarded a horse soldier as a monster half man and half beast; but when both horses and asses had been introduced by the strangers, it was thought most desirable to obtain also some mules which are the common offspring of these two animals. Now, there was a certain chief who possessed a large number both of asses and horses, and he took particular interest in this matter. He knew very well how to breed horses from horses, and asses from asses, but he was not acquainted with the proper method of breeding mules from both; while he was aware that all experiments which are made in the dark, i.e., without the light of previous experience, are both dangerous and uncertain. The consequence was that all his efforts to produce a mule out of a stallion and a she ass were doomed to failure, no doubt because their seeds were not mixed in the right proportion. At last a Sage who was passing that way, and whose insight into the secret working of Nature was infinitely keener and more complete than that of those ignorant people, gave our chief the following advice:

> If you would obtain a mule resembling the
> paternal ass in length of ear and slowness of
> gait, you should feed each of the parents with
> just as large a quantity of food as their nature
> requires. Would you know what this proportion is?
> Give to the male twice as much as to the
> female, then a mare will conceive a mule from
> an ass.

This advice was taken by the chief and, after several failures, his perseverance was crowned with complete success. Nor does it appear contrary to Nature's general plan that two different parents should produce offspring which differs from them both. Look at the leopard, which is said to be the offspring of the leopard and the lioness; in the same way the wolf and bitch beget the lynx; a scion inserted into a good tree produces fruit different from those of the parent stock—new varieties of flowers are obtained by a judicious mingling of the pollen; and the red powder called "our Tincture," being mixed with quicksilver over the fire, produces gold which is utterly unlike either the one or the other. Now, these Americans are able to perform a most singular experiment with metals, and particularly with gold. They have a kind of water in which gold becomes soft like wax and capable of being molded with the hand into any shape they please. This water is not a corrosive, since it does not burn the fingers of those who take up the gold. But we need not doubt that it is some chemical discovery, and that it is obtained by a disuntiling process.... As I could gain no further information in America, I began to think of taking the first opportunity of crossing to Asia: I took with me a very heavy and valuable piece of a certain kind of wood, the most precious I saw here in Brazil, and which is remarkable for its brilliant ebony colour, for this black colour seems proper to America by reason of the blackish poplars and the soil dyed with various hues. The colour of this wood seems to arise from the heat of the sun, and the wonderful peculiarity of the American soil, of which Monandez, that learned physician of Seville, writes as follows: "The variety of colour exhibited by the soil of Peru is most remarkable. If you look at it from a distance, it has the appearance of a patchwork quilt spread out to air in the sun: one part of it is green, another blue, others again are yellow, white, black, and red. Now all these are different kinds of mineral earth: the black earth, if mixed with water or wine, makes an excellent ink, the red soil is said to be the ore of quicksilver, and the Indians paint themselves with it." Well, I took my wood, went aboard a ship, with a white unicorn for its figurehead, and setting sail for Asia, soon arrived in the Persian Gulf.

ASIA: AIR

Asia is the third continent of the world, the continent which answers to the element of Air, and its climate is more temperate than that of the other continents, as it is equally remote from the intense cold of Europe, and the intense heat of Africa. Being both warm and moist, it most admirably corresponds to the element of air; its heat is almost everywhere tempered by the vapours which ascend from the sea. Moist, warm air has fire for its father, and water for its mother, and retains the most active qualities of both its parents. Thus air is a mediator between the two hostile elements, and in its own composition reconciles their strife. In the same way Asia binds Europe (earth) and Africa (fire) together, the grossest and the most subtle of the elements; but without Asia (air) there would be no union between them. By means of air, fire clings gladly to earth, and fosters it; but without air, the fire soon goes out. It is the prerogative and distinctive mark of Asia to be the centre of the world, and to bring forth such fruits as require a warm soft air, as, for instance, dates, balsam, spices of all kinds, and gold itself. Asia is the cradle of our race, the seat of the first Monarchy, the birthplace of our Redeemer. From the Persian gulf I travelled straight through the continent, until I reached those parts of Asia Minor where Jason is said to have obtained the golden fleece. So, being greatly interested in these old world occurrences, I walked out one day to a place said to be the field of Mars, and the site of the Palace of Aetes, the descendant of the Sun; there I met an old man of venerable aspect and authoritative port, who saluted me graciously, and to whom, after returning his salutation, I addressed the following words: "Master, if I am not troubling you too much, kindly enlighten my ignorance, as I can doubt neither your ability nor your willingness to help a stranger." He having signified his willingness to do for me all that lay in his power, I asked him whether those things which were related in history and poetry concerning Jason and his golden fleece, were real facts or mere poetical fictions. He smiled, and made the following reply to my question: "I myself am Jason, and better able than anyone else to give you information concerning those things which have happened to myself. You need not be afraid, for during my lifetime I was no man's enemy, but succoured all, like a good physician; and now that I no longer belong to this world, I am suntil as kindly disposed towards my mortal brethren. On this spot stood the royal seat of my father-in-law, Aetes, whose father was the Sun—not, indeed, that heavenly luminary (which would be incredible), but one like to him in name, and face, and dignity. The golden fleece of the ram, which Mercury had transmuted, and which Aetes had hung in the grove of Mars, I obtained in the following manner: Medea was my chief adviser, and she enabled me by her wise counsel to contend successfully against the fierce and venomous monsters. The watchful Dragon I stupefied with a narcotic, which I cast into his maw; and while he was in that helpless state, I hastened to extract his teeth. These had to be buried in earth first prepared and ploughed up by means of bulls vomiting fire, which fire was extinguished by water poured into their mouths. Then Medea gave me the images of the Sun and Moon, without which, she said, nothing could be done." I asked where I should find all these things. His answer was that he obtained them from Medea, but he could not tell me where she was to be found. "When she left me in her madness," he said, "she was to wedded to old Aegeus, to whom she bore Medus; Medus afterwards went to Asia, and became the founder of the Median race." I wished to ask Jason many more questions, but he excused himself from answering them, and vanished before my eyes. Then I saw that he had been speaking of the Medicine of which I was in search, which also he had shadowed out under the figure of the golden fleece. For the crest of the Phoenix and its feathers are described by the learned as exhibiting a golden splendour. I did not indeed meet with many learned men in Asia; but I was well satisfied to have explored that blessed "aerial earth," especially as Syria and the Holy Land (with their rivers of Adonis and Jordan, in which the leper Naaman was cleansed) form part of it. In Syria, it is related that Adonis was killed by a boar, hounded on by Mars, and that from his wounds there flowed forth that balm by means of which human bodies are preserved from decomposition. On this continent stood the Holy of Holies, into which our Most High Priest entered when He had made atonement for the sins of the whole race on the Cross of Calvary; to Him let us now utter forth the most ardent desires of our hearts in the following prayer:—

> O great and merciful Saviour of the world, Jesus Christ, who being God from all eternity, next madest man in time, in order that, as our Mediator, Thou mightest unite God and man, by satisfying the eternal and infinite

power of God which human sin had provoked to wrath, that is to say, Thyself, the Father, and the Holy Spirit. For this purpose Thou wast born into this world and didst go about doing good among men and didst sanctify this earth by Thy miracles, Passion, Resurrection, and Ascension. To Thee I pray from the very bottom of my heart that as Thou hast given this Medicine for the use of men by ordinary means, and meanwhile hast Thyself cured incurable diseases by Thy Divine power, Who art the Great Physician: so Thou wouldst bestow the gift of this most precious Medicine upon me, the very humblest of thy servants, who for the sake of this most blessed knowledge have taken upon myself so weary a pilgrimage, and so many toils and hardships, as Thou well knowest—in order that I may use it to the glory of Thy Name, and for the relief of my suffering brethren. Thou who art a searcher of hearts, knowest that I despise all worldly pomp, and desire to consecrate my life to Thee, if Thou wilt but work in me both the will and the power of performance: Grant to me the power of exercising boundless charity, of relieving all sufferings, both bodily and mental: Bless me with the gracious gift of Thy Medicine, which comes next in value after the peace of mind and eternal happiness which Thou hast gained for us, in order that its virtue may be effectual in the cure of human sorrow, disease, and pain; to the everlasting praise of the ever-blessed Trinity, world without end, Amen.

When I had poured forth this prayer to the Giver of all good things, I remembered that besides the land which once flowed with milk and honey, but now, under Turkish rule, has become utterly barren and sterile, there was also in Asia, Paradise, which was created for man while he was suntil perfect. Knowing that this blessed garden was situated near Babylon, I journeyed to the spot, but found nothing except a confluence of certain rivers. Thence I travelled to the maritime parts of India, and found a city, called Ormuz, of which there ran a proverb, that if the world was a ring, Ormuz would be its gem. In this city there was a great concourse of eager visitors from the whole neighbourhood; and when I asked one of them whither he was hastening, he said: To the terrestrial paradise. "What," said I, "was I unable to find the ancient garden of Eden, and do these people speak of a new Paradise!" But the man left me standing there, and pursued his journey as fast as he could. While I was considering whether I should follow him, it occurred to me that I should do well to adopt the plan of Columbus, the discoverer of America. So I went to the different gates of the city, and determined to leave it by that one where the sweetest and most fragrant odours were borne towards me on the air. This I did, and I soon found myself on a road where the air was such as might well come from an earthly Paradise, yet was frequented by very few travellers. Ormuz being situated on an island, we soon had to cross a sea, where I saw men fishing up pearls of the purest whiteness. Having obtained some of these for love and money, I had no doubt that I had come into possession of one of the most important substances of the Medicine, for the whiteness of these pearls was such as to defy exaggeration. After pursuing my journey on the mainland, along a very narrow by-path, for some time, I reached a point where two roads met, and there was a statue of Mercury, of which the body was silver while the head was overlaid with gold. The right hand of this statue pointed towards the Earthly Paradise, and when I had followed for some time the road which it indicated, I came to a very broad and deep river, which it was impossible to cross without a boat, though far and wide there was no boat to be seen; but the beauty of the other shore convinced me that it must be the Earthly Paradise. The trees which grew there were covered with golden, orange, citron coloured, purple, and intensely red flowers. There were evergreen laurels, junipers, box-trees, and great store of blossoms of all colours and of the sweetest fragrance: sunflowers, amaranths, lilies, roses, hyacinths, &c. The ear was charmed with the songs and cries of nightingales, cuckoos, parrots, larks, thrushes, and hundreds of other known and unknown birds; nor was there wanting the sweet music of instruments and sweet-toned organs; the taste was gratified, as it seemed, with all manner of delicious fruits, and the fragrance which streamed out on the breeze was such as charmed while it rendered insensible the olfactory nerves of all the people who lived round about, just as the noise of the Nile cataracts becomes inaudible to those who are used to it. But what did the sight of all these glories profit me, who, for want of one little boat, was unable to get at them? So I turned away, with the firm resolution of coming back, as soon as I could do so with a better chance of success; in the meantime, I should be most likely to find the Phoenix that I was in search of, if I crossed over to Africa without further delay. So I directed my course towards the Red Sea, and there landed in Africa.

AFRICA: FIRE

When I reached Africa, more than a year had elapsed from my first setting out; the Sun had once more entered the sign of the Lion, the Moon was at her height in the house of Cancer. All these were circumstances which inspired me with hope. The intense heat of the African climate renders the whole continent torrid, sterile, and dry. It has few rivers, but many wild beasts, which meet together at the riverside, and bring forth among themselves many new and strange shapes, for which Africa is so well known. Satyrs, *cynocephali*, and semi-human beings are said to live there. There are the Mountains of the Moon, and Atlas that bears up the heavens on its shoulders: all these abound in minerals and in serpents. There also is collected the blood of the Dragon which the Dragon has sucked from the Elephant; but when the Elephant falls dead, the Dragon is crushed, and the blood which it has drunk is pressed out of it. Again, in the neighbourhood of the Red Sea, an animal named Ortus has been observed, the colour of whose head is red, with gold lines up to the neck, while its eyes are deep black and its feet white, to wit, the fore feet, but the hind feet are black, the face up to the eyes white—a description which tallies exactly with that which Avicenna gives of our Medicine. Now I heard that not far from the Red Sea there lived a prophetess, named the Erytheraean Sibyl, in a rocky cave; and I thought well first of all to inquire of her concerning this Phoenix. It is she that prophesied and predicted the coming of the Son of God in the flesh. This assertion has indeed been questioned by many writers, but it is borne out by Eusebius, the great historian of the Early Church, and by Cicero. the great orator, who, as is well known, translated this prophecy into the Latin tongue. Abundant evidence to the same effect may also be collected from the works of Virgil, the prince of Roman poets. The passage of Cicero which is referred to by Eusebius, will be found in the second book of his treatise, *De Divinatione* (On Divination). When I came to her, I found her sitting in her cave, which was beautifully overgrown with the spreading boughs of a green tree, and covered with green sod. I saluted her with the lowliest and most deferential humility. At first she seemed somewhat startled at my sudden appearance, and hastily retreated to the interior of the cave. But she was soon won over by my earnest entreaties, and prevailed upon to shew herself at the entrance of her habitation. "Who art thou, stranger?" she inquired, "and what wouldst thou have of me? Dost thou not know that a man may not approach a virgin that dwells in solitude?" "It is not forward boldness that has brought me hither," I replied; "but I have come after mature deliberation, because I feel that it is you, and you alone, that can resolve certain doubts which lie heavy on my mind. If you will shew me this great kindness, I, on my part, promise to do you suit and service, and to fulfill all your commands, as far as lies in my power." When she heard these words, her countenance cleared, and she asked me in a more kindly tone what my business was. "I cannot," she continued, "deny anything to men like you who are anxious to learn." "There are two things," I returned, "concerning which I would crave plain and straightforward instruction from you—namely, whether there was, and is, in these countries of Arabia and Egypt a wonderful bird named Phoenix; whether its flesh and feathers are really an effectual medicine for anger and grief; and, if so, where the bird is to be found?" "The object of your search," she rejoined, "is a great and glorious one; doubt is the first stage of knowledge, and you have also come to the right place and the right person. For the country in which you now find yourself is Araby the Blest, and nowhere else has the Phoenix ever been found; moreover, I am the only person who could possibly give you any definite information about it. I will teach you, and this land will exhibit to you, the glad sight of which I speak. Therefore, listen to my words! Araby the Blest and Egypt have from of old rejoiced in the sole possession of the Phoenix, whose neck is of a golden hue, while the rest of its body is purple, and its head is crowned with a beautiful crest. It is sacred to the Sun, lives 660 years, and when the last hour of its life approaches, it builds a nest of cassia and frankincense, fills it with fragrant spices, kindles it by flapping its wings towards the Sun, and is burnt to ashes with it. From these ashes there is generated a worm, and out of the worm a young bird which takes the nest, with the remains of its parent, and carries it to Heliopolis (or Thebes), the sacred city of the Sun in Egypt. Now, this whole tale which you find in the books of the Ancients is addressed to the mind rather than to the ear; it is a mystical narrative, and like the hieroglyphics of the Egyptians, should be mystically (not historically) understood. An ancient Egyptian writer tells us that the Phoenix rejoices in the Sun, and that this predilection is its chief reason for coming to Egypt. He also relates that his countrymen were in the habit of embalming the Phoenix if it died before its time. If you therefore regard this tale as an allegory, you will not be far wrong; and you know that the flesh and feathers of this bird were of old used in Heliopolis as a remedy for anger and grief." When I heard her say this, I was full of joy, and asked her whether she could tell me how to become possessed of this Blessed Bird and Medicine. She promised not to forsake me, and to do all in her power to help me out of my difficulty. "Nevertheless," she continued, "the most important part of the enterprise must be performed by the toil of your own hands. I cannot describe to you in exact and unmistakable terms the place where the Phoenix lives, yet I will endeavour to make it as plain to you as I may. Egypt, you know, owes all her fertility to the Nile, whose sources are unknown and undiscoverable; but the mouths by which it is discharged into the sea, are sufficiently patent to all. The fourth Son of the Nile is Mercury, and to him his father has given authority to shew you this bird, and its Medicine. This Mercury you may expect to find somewhere near the seven mouths of the Nile; for he has no fixed habitation, but is to be found now in one of these mouths, and now in another." I thanked the Virgin Prophetess most cordially for her gracious information, and at once set my face towards the mouths of the Nile, which are seven:—the Canopic, the Bolbitic, the Sebennitic, the Pelusian, the Tenitic, the Phoenetic and the Mendesic. The way to the Canopic mouth led me through an ancient Christian burial ground, where a most miraculous occurrence is witnessed every year on a certain day in May. From dawn to noon on that day the dead bodies gradually rise from their graves until they are completely visible to the passers by; and from noon to sunset they gradually sink back again into their tombs. If this be true, as eye-witnesses testify, it is a most certain proof of the resurrection of the human body, and exhibits a close analogy to the resuscitation of the dead Phoenix. When I reached the island of Canopus, I inquired where Mercury was to be found. But the people were only hopelessly puzzled by my questions. Some said that, according to Hermes, Egypt exhibits an image of the heavens, and the seven mouths of the Nile (of which the Canopic is the most considerable) correspond to the seven planets, the Canopic mouth they called the habitation of Saturn, the grandfather of Mercury; Mercury was to be found domiciled in some other mouth of the river. At the Bolbitic mouth none of those persons of whom I inquired knew anything about Mercury. Near the third or Sebennitic mouth stood the city of Sebennis, of which the inhabitants were so savage and cruel towards strangers, and so utterly destitute of all the arts and graces of civilization, that I could not conceive of Mercury, the god of culture and science, living in their midst. Moreover, a certain peasant whom I asked whether Mercury's house was there, told me that he had a house in the town but that he never lived there. So I at once went on to the fourth or Pelusian mouth of the file. The famous city of Pelusium is said to have been founded by Peleus, the father of Achilles. It separates Asia and Arabia from Egypt, and was at one time a most wealthy town. When I heard of its greatness in commerce and industry, and of the large quantities of Arabian gold which are imported in this city, one of the wealthiest marts of Egypt, I felt assured that I should find the dwelling of Mercury here; but I was told by the inhabitants that he did not come there very often, though he was received as a most welcome guest whenever he did visit. This answer filled me with dismay, which was in proportion to the hopes which I had conceived, but I determined not to abandon my search until I should have visited the three remaining mouths of the river.

At the Tenitic mouth of the Nile, I learned quite as much as I had learned everywhere else, namely—nothing. When the people who lived there told me that Mercury never came to them at all, I began to bewail my hapless fate, and the many fruitless journeys I had undertaken; and I now saw that perhaps it would have been wiser to have begun at the other end. There, however, I was; only two mouths of the river were left; and in one of these Mercury would be found, if indeed the Prophetess had spoken true. At the Phoenetic mouth another disappointment awaited me. Mercury had once lived there, but had long since migrated somewhere else. At the seventh, or Mendesian mouth, nothing whatever was known about him. It may easily be imagined that, after this long series of disappointments, I began to suspect the Sibyl very strongly of having sent me on a fool's errand, for I had now visited every one of the mouths of the Nile, and yet had not found even a trace of Mercury in any of them. Or if the words of the prophetess had been true, it seemed as if the various people of whom I had inquired must have deceived me with false information. But after more mature consideration of the answers which had been returned to my questions in the different places I arrived at the conclusion that I had merely misapprehended their meaning. So I retraced my steps, and at length succeeded in finding Mercury in one of the mouths, where the people had at first appeared to know nothing about him. He shewed me at great length where I must look for the Phoenix and where I could obtain possession of it. When I reached the place to which he directed me, I found that the Phoenix had temporarily deserted it, having chanced to be chosen umpire between the owl and other birds which pursue it, of which battle we have treated otherwise. It was expected back in a few weeks; but, as I could not afford to wait so long just then, I thought I might be content with the information I had gained, and determined to consummate my search at some future time. So, having returned to my native land, I composed the following epigrams in honour of the Sibyl, Mercury, the Phoenix, and the Medicine.

EPIGRAM

In Honour of the Erythreaean Sibyl, named Herophyle

I thank thee, great prophetess, whose inspiration is not of the fiend, but of the Spirit of God, that thou did direct me on my way to the Son of Nilus, who should shew unto me the bird Phoenix. Full of sacred knowledge, thou did utter forth thy oracles when thou did sing of God who should come in the fashion of a man. Thou dost love Him who, bearing the sentences of highest justice, will be the omnipotent judge of the whole world, though thou wert called a Gentile Maiden, and though men said that thou couldst know nothing of Him. The cave near the Red Sea cannot hold thy greatness, when Christ shall claim thee for His own in Heaven.

EPIGRAM

Dedicated to Mercury of the Sages

The Latins call thee Mercury, the Messenger of the Gods; among the Greeks thy name is that of great Hermes. Thou art called Tenthius on the soil of Egypt; thy father is Nilus, who enriches that soil, and has bequeathed unto thee untold wealth. Thou hast duly conveyed to the peoples of Egypt the laws which Vulcan, being in the secret with thee, has given. All nations of the world behold thee with delight, yet thou desirest to be known to very few. Of how many secrets of Nature have the keys been entrusted to thy keeping! Thy face is red, thy neck is yellow, thy bosom is whiter than purest snow. Thy feet are shod with black sandals, a wand with a double snake in no wise hurts thy hand. This is thine apparel whereby thou art known to all, O Hermes! Thy complexion is fittingly of four hues. Thou did shew to me the glorious bird Phoenix by the mouth of an interpreter, and I thank thee for thy love with all my heart; though the words be light, they are weighty with gratitude.

AN EPIGRAM

In Praise of the Phoenix

O Marvel of the World, prodigy without a blot, unique Phoenix who givest thyself to the great Sages! Thy feathers are red, and golden the hues of thy neck; thy nest is built of cassia and Sabaean frankincense. When thy life is drawing to a close, thou knowest the secret way of Nature by which thou art restored to a new existence. Hence thou gladly placed thyself on the altar of

Thebes, in order that Vulcan may give thee a new body. The golden glory of thy feathers is called the Medicine of health, and the cure of human woe. Thou has power to cast out disease and to make the old young again. Thee Blessed Bird, I would rather have than all the wealth of the world, and the knowledge of thee was a delight which I sought for many years. Thou art hidden in the retreat of thine own nest, and if Pliny writes that he saw thee in Rome, he does greatly err. Thou art safe in thy home, unless some foolish boy disturb thee:—if thou dost give thy feathers to anyone, I pray thee let him be a Sage.

On the Hermetic Medicine of the Phoenix

If all the mountains were of silver and gold, what would they profit a man who lives in constant fear of death? Hence there cannot be in the whole world anything better than our Medicine, which has power to heal all the diseases of the flesh. Wealth, and riches, and gold, all yield the prize to this glorious possession: and whoever does not think so, is not a man, but a beast.

If anyone will not acknowledge the force of reason, he must needs have recourse to authority.

For a Complete List of Publications,
Please address:
Holmes Publishing Group LLC
Postal Box 2370
Sequim WA 98382 USA